The Sadness of Days

Selected and New Poems

Luis Omar Salinas

Arte Publico Press
Houston

This volume is made possible through support from the National Endowment for the Arts, a federal agency, and the Texas Commission on the Arts.

Arte Publico Press
University of Houston
Houston, Texas 77004

Library of Congress No. 85-073348
ISBN 0-934770-58-1

Printed in the United States of America

for my father

Contents

Crazy Gypsy (1970)

Afternoon of the Unreal (1980)

Prelude to Darkness (1981)

Darkness Under the Trees (1982)

Walking Behind the Spanish (1982)

The Sadness of Days, *new poems*

Acknowledgements

The author is grateful to the following presses which published his poems
in book form: Origenes Publications, Abramas Publications, Mango, and
the Chicano Studies Library Publication Unit at UC-Berkeley.

Crazy Gypsy

Through the Hills of Spain

for Miguel Hernandez

Through the hills of Spain
among the flowers and the seeds of life
a train wanders

Hernandez . . . Hernandez

the night is hushed
mockingbirds listen
to the tirades of men
wounded in battle

blood of your blood
senseless death in the air
the wind swallows birds

Hernandez . . . Hernandez

There is death caught by the nostrils
    of the sky
there is death everywhere
the sea calling to forlorn travelers

Hernandez . . . Hernandez

your wound leaves the redness of
    skies never conquered
untouched, virginal

Oh yawning tenderness
lust on the wheels of a train
blood on the faces of bulls
soil calloused by murder
homicide of undertakers
and children

Swords of the flesh Alicante
ripe years of manhood
Oh dawning life
overpowering weatherworn axes
heaven of your life

Hernandez . . . Hernandez

Through the hills of Spain
among the flowers and the seeds of life
a train wanders

Mexico, Age Four

I

on the corner near my house
   is a churro factory
      and the free man sleeps
how ugly the air smells in this town
   as if torn hair and blood
      were on the paving stones,
and taxi drivers sleep on their meters
   sluts
drink iced tea through the shattered
   windows
  I see only
    hungry beggars and sheep
      on their knees

II

traveling through a cemetery in Saltillo
   I find a truth as terrible
     as murder
belly buttons and taciturn devils
    paint the walls
      of MEXICO
and I can no longer see pain
   only the drip of the water
    on a leaky rooftop

III

the dogs bark
   at every doctor and drunken cop
the moonlight gathers in the stoic
   leaves of autumn

IV

and I take heaven as my ally
and sleep soundly
through the haunted
screams
of night
as cold as mud
and sighs of love
as deep
as pig grunts
silenced by their masters

Aztec Angel

I

I am an Aztec angel
 criminal
  of a scholarly society
 I do favors
  for whimsical magicians
 where I pawn
  my heart for truth
 and find my way
  through obscure streets
 of soft-spoken
  hara-kiris

II

I am an Aztec angel
 forlorn passenger
  on a train
 of chicken farmers
  and happy children

III

I am the Aztec angel
 fraternal partner
  of an orthodox society
 where pachuco children
  hurl stones
 through poetry rooms
 and end up in cop cars
 their bones itching
  and their hearts
 busted from malnutrition

IV

I am the Aztec angel
    who frequents bars
    spends evenings
    with literary circles
    and socializes with spiks
    niggers and wops
        and collapses on his way
        to funerals

V

Drunk
    lonely
        bespectacled
    the sky
        opens my veins
          like rain
        clouds go berserk
        around me
    my Mexican Ancestors
        chew my fingernails

I am an Aztec angel
    offspring of a woman
        who was beautiful

Burial

I am to attend a burial today
    and on an alleyway on the moon
where my mind lies scattered
    over an ocean
as a rose in a cobweb
as snow on a young girl's hair
a storm awakens trains
that carry silence on their backs
and dead children who were
supposed to go to purgatory
in their arms
my eyes are singing loudly
flowers grow on moons
God is whistling on a train
and my childhood friends
    are playing games
The faces of weather-worn skulls
hang loosely on the wind
    the night with eagle's claws
    has torn the flesh
    of artichoke intestines
the burial was supposed to be
    a fantasy
where childhood dreams
and sheepherders
talk about the distant
    sea
but now the horrible pain
    keeps me silent
this Tuesday in November
    as the cold earth
    feels meek
    and expectant as a pregnant
    mother

And I carry the news
    to my Mexican friends
    and I carry my soul
    to my America
    as blood from a cloud
    as blood from the earth
    runs through my veins

Sunday . . . Dig the Empty Sounds

It is Sunday, and I look for you
a meteor wandering, lazy,
simple as dust. I've encountered life here,
a single shadow discovering the breast.
I bake the joys of afternoons in the sun,
with the blood of children
running weakly through the street
struck dumb by dark.

The human eyes of women loiter
here like stars on the cobblestones—
water of the oppressed
standing still on the horizon
caught like a fish in the narrow heart
of mice . . .

The human mouths of clouds
go by here
running thieves in the sunlight.

I survive the rain
dreaming, lost, frowning
the shoes of my mother
talking
to the children in Africa
to the crazy dogs
that huddle in corners
starving
empty of sound.

Saturday

It is Saturday . . . day of apples and turnips
on heavy trucks that pass my aunt's house
sleeping. My cousin is awake quibbling with
his painful back, this corner of the earth
surrenders to the anarchy of cows.

We are off to see the movies and the flesh
of night is torn into small, little children
as angels eat breaded clouds and spiders
tell stories to the rabbits of the neighborhood.

Nights and Days

I am alone
and with me
the roads
as empty containers

if you become
saddened
by suffering
butterflies

look to the right
and you see a town
on the other side
where the neighbors
hide themselves
like swallows
working in hell
for low pay

I could have
imagined this
world before
but not this
night of darkness

not this night.

21

Crazy Gypsy

I

I am Omar
  the crazy gypsy
    nimble footed
      and carefree

    I write poems
      on walls
        that crumble
        and fall

    I talk to shadows
      that sleep
        and go away
          crying

    I meet fearless girls
      who tell me
        their troubles
          my loneliness
            bottled up in their
            tummy

II

I am Omar
  the crazy gypsy
    I write songs
      to my dead mother
        hurl stones
          at fat policemen
            and walk on seaweed
            in my dreams

    I walk away from despair
      like a horse walks away

from his master
end up in jail
eating powdered eggs
for breakfast

III

My spine shakes
to the songs
of women

I am heartless and lonely
and I whistle a tune
out of one of my dreams

where the world
babbles out loud
and Mexican hat check girls
do the Salinas Shuffle
a dance composed
by me in one
of my nightmares
and sold
for a bottle
of tequila

IV

I am Omar
the crazy gypsy
I waltz through avenues
of roses
to the song
of Mariachis

V

I am Omar
the Mexican gypsy
I speak of love
as something whimsical and aloof
as something naked and cruel

I speak of death
  as something inhabiting
      the sea
    awkward and removed

I speak of hate
    as something nibbling my ear . . .

Afternoon Of The Unreal

Going North

for my grandfather

Those streets in my youth,
hilarious and angry,
cobblestoned by Mestizos,
fresh fruit
and dancing beggars.
Gone are the soldiers
and the nuns.
My Portuguese friends
have gone North.
The school girls
have ripened
overnight.
I hum Spanish tunes
waiting for the bus
in Fresno.
These avenues
I watch carefree
young, open collared
like my grandfather
who died in a dream
going North.

I Go Dreaming Serenades

I dream the afternoon
how many times I've
searched for romance
and found the bib
of silence.

I'm opposed to the muse
keeping something from me.
I always wanted to be
immortal.
Funny how things happen.
I assumed everyone was.

That is until
the incomprehensible
came out of nowhere
with its face
of troubled darkness
and lies danced like pigeons
to the tune of my misery.

Damn truth is I can't read
while I'm asleep
and that's as true a statement
I've made all day.
Haven't seen anything different
from last night
except I woke up feeling heavy.

I sacrifice this bitterness
with your wet kisses
plunging like devils.
I've gained the scholar's
sobriety and aloofness
and dismiss this heartache.

Next time I see you
a cold wind will bite your
nipples and sing;
or go crazy like your
spindrift eyes,
which wrecked me
through a cruel winter.

The Boats

for Henri Coulette

Somnolent
they appear
as insects
on top of the sea.

Passengers
in them
look like gentle
misanthropes
on vacation from dusty homes.
I wish I could
sleep as gently
as these wooden dreamers
who pursue pleasure
and go everywhere
on impulse—
doctors and surgeons of the sea.

And how nice to ease
into love
fancy-eyed and happy,
leaving behind this very much
beaten and tired heart.
It's true, on a day like this,
anything is possible.

Seagulls ascend,
clouds speak,
among the rocks fishermen
bait their hooks;
bikini clad girls
cross my path
full breasted and drowsy . . .
I raise this glass to them,

to the boats and the suitcases
and the flags in the wind—

Here's to life, amigos,
this life that jumps
and brings an army.

Here's to the sea
that hangs on,
and to the sun also—silver colored,
clouded,
walking like an old man.

Ambitious Anarchist

He eats up life
like a red ripe plum,
chasing the girls,
wanting a time
with the earth.
Politics, he scoffs,
meat for the devil.

I for one eat ripe plums,
chase girls
and amble into history
like a lame horse.
I also bet on horses
and watch the sunlight
touch the forehead
of this dark world,
giving thanks.
I'm such an ambitious
anarchist
I haven't got a goddamned
thing to live for
except my poems
and the girls and horses.
I strike a match,
light my cigarette
and whistle like the shuffling
feet of nuns in a monastery:
Learning to live again, he says
between gulps of beer.

For Armenia

I feel enchantment every time
I enter an Armenian household.
Their daughters, you know . . .
I am the kibitzer of chatter
in the kitchen, companion
to the baying of firepans
and doors.

Here I am. Poet and vagabond
eating tacos in Armenia,
in the house of Shish-Kabob
and Kings. I tell them
I am the descendant of
Cuauhtemoc and the evening
gathers like knives in the moonlight.

I drink coffee, eat baklava
and the night air comes in
singing to the tune of dusted
stars, hovering above
like mad gypsies.
I want to tell them
I'm off on a gretchen
mission of immortality
as I abandon rainbows,
universities and dictionaries.
But I falter like a fatal Aztec
ghost, and condemn dreams.
I leave, rousted off to the
mountain of languages
stuffed with life and secrets.
And what awaits me is the future—
blue ringing of flesh—
as I waltz,
a man like any other,
watching everything emerge
like a crazy wake.

alinas Sends Messengers to the Stars

Sir. You understand. I am poor.
I work from sunup to sundown.
Never mind what I do . . .
yet, I'll tell:
I send messengers to the stars.

With all the trouble and madness
on this earth
I feel the stars to be
more human.
I think I'll weave
blankets
and tell them
I love them so dearly.

Ode to the Mexican Experience

The nervous poet sings again
in his childhood voice, happy,
a lifetime of Mexican girls
in his belly, voice
of the midnoon bells
and excited mariachis
in those avenues persuaded out
of despair.

He talks of his Aztec mind,
the little triumphs and schizoid trips,
the many failures
and his defeated chums
dogs and shadows,
the popularity of swans in his neighborhood
and the toothaches of rabbits
in the maize fields.

I know you in bars
in merchant shops,
in the roving gladiators,
in the boats of Mazatlan that never anchor,
in the smile of her eyes,
in the tattered clothes of school children,
in the never-ending human burials;
those lives lost in the stars
and those lost in the stars
and those lost in the wreckage
of fingernails,
the absurd sophistry of loneliness
in markets, in hardware stores,
in brothels.

The happy poet talks in his sleep,
the eyes of his loved one
pressing against him—

her lips have the softness
of olives crushed by rain.

I think of the quiet nights
in Monterrey
and of my sister who woke me up
in the mornings.

The soft aggressive spiders
came out to play in the sunlight,
and suffering violins in pawn shops,
hell and heaven and murdered angels
and all the incense of the living
in poisoned rivers
wandering aimlessly amid dead fish,
dead dreams, dead songs.
I was an altar boy,
a shoeshine boy,
an interventionist in family affairs,
a ruthless connoisseur of vegetables,
a football player.
To all the living things I sing
the most terrible and magnificent
ode to my ancestry.

Magnificent Little Gift

To friends with troubles

I collapse
into the awareness
that life has
been fighting me.
The question is:
From what corner
of the room shall I slash
its grim victorious smile?

My feet ache from walking.
I rebel, slowly turning
into the corridors of the mind
believing I'm an angel.

Yesterday I lived like a bird.
Today I adore roses.
Tomorrow I'll weep
looking at the white bones
of mountains.

Maybe if I remember
the dying
I'll be all right.

I have a dog that follows me
from room to room
like a doctor.
The wives of the moon
sit silent.
A berserk seagull dances
on the shore.

I live the music in me
gazing at a train that never stops
tripping into bars
thinking of churches
and dancing with a girl
with the heart of an angel
the eyes of a dove
the arms of a madonna.

As I said, life is fighting me.
I shall aim a blow at its ears
breathing poetry
counting stars in the evening
floating with the universe
thanking God for this gift
this life.

Salinas Is on His Way

Go, friends, quickly to your tasks and wives.
This night I have to discover the clouds—
talk to the galaxies.
My parents are old
and the road is a serpent full of ambitions.
And what remains of me after sleep
is sunlight entering
like a nun into church.
After dreams get through with me
I shall devour books, sing arias,
walk on snow,
have arguments with darkness
and crawl into the corner of the sea
listening to the tingle of bells,
What remains of me after sleep
may be a corpse.
So send out word:
Salinas is on his way—
quoting verses from the Bible,
making a mad dash through the night,
making certain everything is secure.

Drunk Cemeteries

There are drunk cemeteries
in my heart
walking on dark roads in the evening
or beating my fist in the fog
or gagging my pillow
they lie there
with the sound of dogs or bells or wounded shoes
drinking the blood of my ancestry
sitting with wild geese
intent on silence
perhaps they remind us of lost childhoods
or of the pages of worn out books
there is almost always someone there
to call out
the kisses of earth
towns hide there
the fragrance of flowers
the subtle mouth of a woman
the doorknobs of rich houses
I could talk all day of this
while swans look into mirrors
and the mothers of butterflies
whisper into ears of stone
but I've had enough

On a Friend Who Drowned
and Whose Body Was Never Recovered

First your child
an accidental bullet
pronounced dead
before your eyes

I can think
of voyages
and stars
that will never
be seen
and of the many silences
between you and them

Somehow you faced
your family
your son's blood
still in your eyes

You drowned
not three weeks
later
you who worked
with the acid
of Mexico
on your face

On your back
the toughness of your spirit showing
so we all said
in cantinas
with the music
of women in the early morning
turning the drums in our brains

We composed poems with the common
breath of our survival
running as if to catch a shadow
and like the restless relatives
that we were not
we helped each other

friend of work
friend of the night
friend of childhood

As this night comes to an end
the trumpets of the mariachi are silent
and the many worlds you were
trumpet your name at dawn.

May your eyes turn to butterflies
and let them swim Oh God
into the sunlight of another life

On a Windy Night in Monterrey, Mexico

I am made stupid
by the squalor
and the painted dummies
of meat in the market.

Sitting at the table
of Las Noches restaurant
I send the shoeshine boy
      for a bottle.

The night has the intensity
of a girl being raped
      by her landlord,
and I envision a shop
with nude women
      calling to be laid.

The girls at the other table
      are giddy with laughter.
The insides of my girl
      companion
swell like onions,
her dress doesn't fit
but neither does the waitress's,
her stubby toes speak
      of greater days—

and last night
I dreamed that I spoke to
      the Virgin Mary
and the night before
I was having headaches
      over the ignorance
of my beautiful Mestizo people.

Maybe tomorrow I'll go swimming
in Don Diego's quinta
and won't have to worry
    about my dreams.

The days of Conquerors
and talking horses
    are over.
I'll see if my companion has ears.
I've got a lot of things
    to talk about
here on this windy night
    in Monterrey.

Many Things of Death

Death today
smells
of apples
worms chewing
their gums

a child with mud
on his hands

today it has
the mouth of an insect
crawling through
the avenues

it has the nightmares
of fish
drunk on rain

it has the footsteps
of a gardener
wanting to murder
a chair
it has nonsense
in its eyes
a dog barking
at a cloud

a woman opening
an awkward door

it has the stubbornness
of an owl hatching
its eggs

it has the elegance
and laughter
of clowns

many things of death
in the taciturn
protest
of ants in the unrest of flies

Visions of Flowers

(a love wish)

She talks of long journeys
into dust, the crumpled
dresses in the field, the sun
tearing her thighs and
breasts—oval rounded machines
that feed the village
and swallow hard at making
a living.
I, in turn, enter her life
with ten dollars, simply,
like wooden snow in the field
where heaven's bitch-stars
watch her undress.
Her eyes show the magic
of her God, and the strong
crotch and defeated breasts
work for a song.

Olivia

I walk on the edge
of my mother's grave
sadly touching the rain
as if it were her dress
disguised as silk.
I wander on, a shadow
speaks as softly
as my hands
and we must leave off
where it began
the coughing
and my four year old
arms ready to please.
Mother, you have
made the cold into fire
and your beauty the talk
of the town
I know death like I know
you, mother,
leavened bread in the oven,
a dog,
my sister Irma,
and the neighbors
wailing like our kitchen.
I didn't come to this world
to be frightened
yet your death sticks
in my stomach
and I must clean the kitchen
with my hands
and I must wander on
into the night of leavened bread
and pursue truth
like a tube needing air.

Until Heaven Gets Tired

In this curious mad evening
when the things I invent
are unreal and my life, like a cow,
sings crudely, I make the villages
in my brain whistle at the girls.
There are drums and flutes,
women milking shadows
in this fleeting residence.
I leave my prayers here
in this palace of bad stomachs,
my heart is young again
and I pick up my faces,
Mexican madness,
tequila and flowers
raining down from heaven.
What wild dream is this?
These hands of mine groan.
I toss them at the wind.
It is the sea I listen to,
these carcasses and cunts
stealing nectar from the dreaming stars.
I must have drunk a mad star
or dreamed this dream.
This life
so difficult to understand!
Let's chase ghosts
and dance with women in the street,
frolic in the dawn until heaven
gets tired of looking at our dirty faces.

Poem for Charles Warrington Moulton

You are reading a book
with an oak-like intensity—
your body leather-like, poised,
a coffee cup in your hand.

Earlier we were discussing
the copulating habits of flies,
and how, yes how they do it
so uncannily.

There's a hemisphere full of flies
orbiting heaven like choir girls,
breasts open to the clouds.
You close an eye and wish.

A child could tell you
more about flies.
Yes a child with the heart
of a grape swallowed in the night.

Let's wait for the reincarnation
of flies, Charles.
And stop reading that book
and listen to this poem
which will gain in due time
the importance of a fly.

And reincarnate into your coffee cup.

A Beautiful Nun's Sorrow

I am here.
I touch my chin and
a flight of sparrows.
leaves the heart.

I am now looking
at the plump roundness
of an orange,
and ache for its sweetness.
That I would like to plunge
my hands into a beautiful nun's
almond blossoming breasts—
offer her a delectable peach
for penance.

Could she understand the cock
of a poet. Would she think
the devil had entered her life
to unscrew her lovely head
into perdition?
Who knows? I only know what
I feel in this idiosyncratic
flight of fancy.
I have been moved to a sorrow,
her sorrow, pained hearing
its own echo—
moving gently through the heart
like a huge spear.

I Jig Lightheaded

That I'm a piece of thought
wandering loose through
the street, and that a smile
comes at me hiding in my brow.

That I don't know what drives
the night into the palm
of a cat's paw and snickers
away like a flamenco.

That a songster comes at me
with a stick denouncing
my shoes, and lust creeps
in before breakfast.

And my anger walks between
two lepers, or a woman wants
my body and I delude her
with romantic logic.

I look for little miracles
here and there, stick
them in my pockets
and appear unannounced
at a funeral.

And this brain counts twos
and threes and can't save
me; five, six, seven
and I jig lighheaded,
"What's there to worry about?"

Good Night

The good night settles in,
the stars hover above
like happy nuns, and I'm
as unsettled as the restless
finches that gather in
this cloudless night.
Sailing through doubts
which light into prayer
and go with the sea
like sailors.

I'm an unhappy troubadour
hewing thoughts in the darkness;
expecting the ghost
or watching for meteors.
The liberated lady has left
with her Baudelairean guitar,
strumming damnation—
I go passionless under the stars.

Dreaming serenades, inventing
love affairs, waiting—
hoping for a blue ringing
of songs to make better
nights of my troubles.

Prelude To Darkness

The Muse Goes Daydreaming

The muse goes on—
whistling concertos . . .
She has taken my shirt
and made a bed,
talks to my shoes
as my lovers.
She has ruffled my hair
and danced around, giddy
with tongue.
I asked her to leave.

Today, she came back with
my poem, laughing
like the sunlight.
I beat her black and blue.
She rolled over dead,
saying, "Quit your daydreaming."

Salinas Sees Romance Coming His Way

for B.H.

With dreams coming my way baptized
in the sweetheart waters of moonlight,
a gypsy moon with your petulant face
is at once dolorous and given
to the higher reaches of the stars.
A story lays unfolding
in virgin and phosphorescent scrolls,
a tale where the lover takes you away
on his tiny boat of memories, bemused,
crazy with the passion of brooms, candlesticks,
lifting your breasts to his mouth of cymbals . . .

    with my fingers I open the roads on your hands
    and lead them to strum flowers and liken the wind
    to a fortune teller blowing in our ears
    the soft promises of October.
    I want to take you to a cemetery of seagulls,
    open you like a bible, incandescent fruit,
    and read you our poetry, a memory that hovers
    above with the dark feet of a magnificent night.

After Basho

Blissful, bashful and with obligations
I go offending reality
with the smile of little
misfortunes.

Imbecile Lament

Child that can't think

to the Spanish poets

I wish to tell someone
my heart has gone
out of doors, in its suit
of silver, ragged and pained.
And that my waltzing mind
has nowhere to go anymore.
But this afternoon zooms in
with its lies and insults,
and I don't know.
What if life appeared anew?
With a plate of snow?
In the nude like a strange
woman?
If the night would turn
into a swallow and go
begging?
If the world turned
its face upward
and never saw me?
I would go to the cemetery
and throw something
at the devil.

empty of life poor man a lot of pain

doesn't have a creative nature

The Nuns Too Would Be Proud

Aquinas would be proud
of me, even though I
haven't been laid
in four months.
I am a most determined
scholar, and after pinning
a flower on a woman,
I kiss her, weakly confident
I will see her again.
I will see her sweetly melancholy,
determined herself
to see me famous, surrounded
by good company and plenty
of money. A poet quietly
singing his cosmos
to the unfortunate.
A beautiful woman has a way
of getting at the blood,
of filling one's spirit,
and in spite of the odds
I remain good natured
ready to look at the sunlight
of every day which comes
around the corner at me
like the great millionaire
I'll never be.

In a Foggy Morning

Students amble in
with co-ed winter fashions,
the university is wide awake and I
sit in my blue Picasso coat with a
stack of Christmas cards, composing
one line, or two, looking at
the blank stares from beauty.

On a day like this anything could
have meaning—a walk through campus,
a cup of coffee, the turn of a collar
on a gardener could mean I will
be saved from the obscurity of letters.

But this day I have to decide
what I want to do with myself;
I could sit here forever watching the
sunlight beat me into rags, or salute
the yellow leaves with something
to keep us both from falling
into bits of sadness. I wish I could.
I've been sad lately and yet in love.
In a sense, her face comes toward me,
the sun banks snow on the mountains
and calls me like her absence.
So I come to school, ready
for these few blue lines,
waiting for the fog to lift
so I can see myself folding these
hands and arms like a blanket.

Last Tango in Fresno

Midnoon and I'm between
a pastrami and a dream.
In love with bad love
I put out my cigarette
and count my blessings.
Bad kharma and no lover.
I want to seduce
the nearest woman
and run off to the nearest motel.
But the nearest woman
is thinking of vegetables
and buying a gift
for her lover.
So I waltz down
the avenue,
feeling great and important
and bump into
a lesbian friend
who is out of
work and needs a job.
I give her five bucks
and feel
that in the next life
I'll get it all back.

I Go Voyaging Afternoons

(listening to Pedro Infante)

"I was born in the nude
                    with no inheritance"
and walked birdlike
                    into the afternoon
        singing melancholic verses.
My lifelong ambition has been
                                to cross the ocean
        with a good woman.
                        On the corner of my life
I lay myself like a lark dancing
                            for my betrothed
who dreams nightingales.
                        I should have been a ventriloquist
I catch her lips
            like falling rainbows.
I feel like I'm visiting someone
                            who is no longer there.
It is like the afternoon
                        waiting for dusk to clear.
On the corner of my life
                    I wait for my dream,
my troubadour friends
                    drink like crazy,
        I enjoy good wine,
and go voyaging afternoons,
                            through rain, loneliness,
roads,
        half sunlight,
                    and
                        hopes.

I Sigh in the Afternoon

I sigh in the afternoon deep
in my suit,
blue with absence;
        a serenade of poems
        cutting the air,
bending to pick up life
out of its doggerel sleep.

Dewy-eyed madrigals,
    hewing magic
  in the corner
    of a barrio.

And the music of winter
    jumping in the nude,
        like a woman.

If strutting the boards
        brought her peace
and if smiling
        through motherhood
brought her joy,
        what can I offer?

And I've been cutely
        turning my eyes into
dark forests of women
        who reappear faraway
in their slavery.

I drift through promiscuity
        like a hungry dove
carrying my leaden heart
        like driftwood
            through the haze.

I peck away at life
    chiseling
        "something."

II

Could it be bereavement
    dressed in gaudy rags,
or the advent of some dream
    coming into the brain
from the dribble and patter
    of poverty?

Or the invention of some Utopia
    where the arctic nipple finds
        solace?
The women in my life
are boats leaving
    and coming
and the ocean
    is so deep.
And the night air smells
        of Lesbians.

III

And I've been smiling too long
    to be overworked
        and underpaid.
I've got to find someone
        to talk to.
I have a ruthless rendezvous
        with humanity,
and I will not rest half-ignorant
    in the cubicle of thought,
alienated from the happy condition
        which plagues man.
I'm learning to question
    psychiatry psychology
    the label given to genius.
I will fight everywhere—
I am questioning the modern term

man.
We have to take a scrutinizing
    look, a deep haunting courageous
      blissful look into the mirror
    of our ways, or
our crazy souls will not rest.

Prelude to Darkness

It would be nice to have something
to say for a change, I tell myself.
The night air listens like a Christian.
And I count the shadows
in my yard like the great crustaceans
out to enliven me.
Sunlight leaving again,
my worries creating misery—
a young night appears
and once more I go on the edge . . .

        Pedro Infante's singing
        "Tu Solo Tu" and
        the country girls who dance
        once a week and go to church
        are leaving the Rainbow Ballroom
        on the strong arms of Jorge Negrete . . .

Who could have dreamed this
agony up? The nuns
with their sorrowful mysteries
and dark beads? Jesus
with a bad memory?

It Was Sunday

It isn't easy
    coming back from madness,
    I told her.
There was a sad sky overhead
and stars were composing
a song.
I reached for her
    and knew there and then
    we would have to be
    two people in the shower
    and forget the gossip.
    It was a Sunday
    to be ourselves—
                drinking lite beer,
                smoking cigarettes
                reading the bible,
                and talking about
                    the dead
                in a motel
                where everyone
                sleeps and discusses
                the high temperatures.

An unforgettable Sunday
    and we drank
and shut out the light;
    that evening the world seemed
        to be dancing,
and somewhere there was a tune
        for lovers
who wanted to be just themselves
    in a world with too much
giddiness and things
            taken for granted.

I felt like a pheasant
        had just been flushed
over my shoulder,
        and stared into the cosmos
        wanting to make a crazy
        story out of love.

This Is About the Way It Should Be

I listen to the frantic philosophy
of swallows on forgotten Tuesdays
at our reunion where everyone
appears to be drunk, idly
moved with indifference,
or sadly scratching.
I am then reminded
of my poor manners,
posthumous remarks on literature
and the avant-garde.
I am told repeatedly
that I am crazy, that I make
a poor husband, and that
I will end a bad death.

I will all this to Seville,
Toledo, my home state
and all the illegitimate
children I wish I'd had.
I give all this to the Politico
who eulogized my name
without knowing I was still
alive and writing.
And last of all I give
this poor rendering
of my emotional state
to a woman who wants
everything, even my shoes.

Watching it Move

I appear
dogbeaten
amid beer
and the promise
of the future.
Here I am
out of work,
disconsolate,
enamored of birds,
ready to take flight
myself.
But the future sits
on all fours,
singing like a gypsy,
and I hand faith
an embrace
and hope the
best is coming
like Christ.
I've been strangely
moved by a woman,
and like the coming
together of a dream,
I'm here.
There's no clemency
in pain,
only the memory
of my mother's death
pricks me
and I rise
to chores
a little less
ignorant of the past,
waiting like a child
on the pier,
watching the stars

overtake the sky
and thank God
I haven't taken
my own life.

By the Elms

I don't know myself today,
and this winter aches
from above; it is a hurting
of the night air,
of anxious swallows
daring into me like
philosophers.
I want to sit down
to a mother, let up
and find something.
I want to begin
as mourner, end up
lover. Crowd into
the corner of a finger,
and be seduced somewhere.
I want to take this
bag of bones to an
unimportant subway,
and these eyes to
a promising woman.
My heart is walking
on all fours, raw boned.
I'm tired of grunting
romances,
of quiet lovers' burials
by the elms where the
birds are singing.

As Evening Lays Dying

Enraptured
as the evening lays dying
with the classical
music of your eyes, dancing
in the wind; I offer
what little I have
to you, childless woman
of hope. I smite this
solitude into a giving
of sorts. And ponder
whether it is the magic
of gods, or the smattering
of bliss like the plum blossoms
sprayed white in wind
which preordained
to make me love you.
And feel each passing
day, like gypsies,
while I feel orphanages
in the sky and
in my thumbs singing.
As the evening lays dying,
I announce this heart
for all its irony,
and venture forward
into the world,
poetic and unassuming.

Romance in the Twilight

for B.H.

Night falls like a romantic
in your arms, I'm tasting
air and October's nipples.
Your eyes closed now,
the world small, tiny
in a room where the smell
and perfume of your body
has me upraised, ready
to perform miracles.

It's been heaven
I think to myself,
my luck so magnificent—
now I'm wondering if you're
ready to leave, and when
you do, a thud is there
louder than your eyes.

You're most unusual;
when I hold you,
subtle animal
with the most delicate
touches to your soul.

It seems I can't
invent anyone else,
the clouds have me,
the emotion is ours
and it's all we have;
learn to trust
this devil
whose heart knocks
birds to their death.

Darkness Under The Trees

I Go Dreaming Roads in My Youth

I'm not interested in the poverty
of ignorance and its songs,
to be generous to myself is my song;
I will give my shirt to no one
even though I talk too much and
give my words to the ungrateful
they will not find a home in my thoughts.

I put on my hat, stride forward,
act, dream, love; I take a drink
and let fame touch me, yet in the end
I'll place it to rest.

When I raise my arm to the populace
I raise it with sincerity
and pride in my monstrous vitality.
When the world clubs me
I shall fight back, if it loves me
I will love back, if it steps in my
shadow's fortune, I will give thanks
to God and those who surround me.

I have many stories, a haughty dramatist
weaving scenes of optimism, of alegria,
of romance. The world is too tired
and little concerned with pathos or
the consequences of tragedy.
What is important is the eloquence
of a river and a boy pushing a boat
into the water, a white dove gently
from the hands of his mother and
a clumsy serenade dreaming the afternoon.

Today, I like this world, and
if your life is worth nothing, don't sing,
don't come to my door with broken hearts
and complaints. Today, I go dreaming
roads in my youth.

I'm On My Way

Evening becomes evening,
and I'm not letting up, God.
I'm still sleeping
with my neighbor's wife
on Sundays—
and sometimes drive nails
into flowers out of boredom
and bump into beggars
when morning goes dead.
Oh, mischief like a thief
cutting roses, presenting
them to choir girls . . .
I'll make it
to heaven on a motorbike yet—
beardless Leo Da Vinci
singing Spanish folk songs.

Salinas Wakes Early
and Goes to the Park to Lecture Sparrows

Little philosophers
of the twig,
gaunt adventurers of philanthropy,
you understand I'm from sturdy
merchant stock.

I've taken violin lessons
from the trash collector,
six lessons in six weeks,
and I sold it and turned to you
hard workers of the light.

I turn down the road
beating the dust
from my coattails,
dust that smells of you.

Beaks like musicians
looking for work,
I'm reminded of far off
music from a girl's lips
drawn to your sounds
under the October sky.

I woke early to remind
you of your chores
little pay and sadness,
of your duties to God
and lovers.

Now I'm off to study chess
and bellies of cows dreaming milk.
And like the mariachi
I look at the sun,
drum a gourd
and go dreaming into the afternoon

happy to unfold this spirit
which aches from the ashes
of sweat and moonlight.
I adore your freedom
and when unhappy
watch your flight
into my dark conjecturing.

I Toss Smiles toward the Open Sea

What is happening to me?
I ask as love
builds its fingers
of snow over my heart.

It is like the raindrops
of silk over a woman
who smiles often
and is fortunate
at dusk.

And I pale over the window
of life, waiting by the elms
for the sparrows that
spring from my heart
into the night air.

Air of guitars
and deaf mutes,
air of laughter
knifed in the air
by swallows
who understand
my loneliness.

Into the night of darkness
and pirates, drummers off
to Europe, I create delight
and smile towards the open sea,
calm, like a stranger
grieving a little,
out to sea for the last
time.

Coming Back from It

I've been thinking about falling
in love, but the weather has been harsh,
a hair shirt of sorts, some ashes,
and I've noticed
a blind leaf fall on my black boots.
I catch my breath, lift
my white handkerchief up to my face
and look at my palm, where ambition crosses
and recrosses like the traffic at 5:00.

The cat from up the street
breaks toward a bird
and the sunlight catches
at my pulse
like a leaf puzzled in the air.

In Mazatlan

(After a vision of Shelley being cremated
at the edge of the Mexican coast)

Being a bachelor is crazy business,
        in Mazatlan I thought I was the Mexican
        Shelley. And casting glances
            at the Primavera seagulls
        I lost myself there—
            like a deep afternoon sky.
I left my heart
        standing among the people
        in their revolution
                of joy
        and dog-beaten
                saludos.
My bones singing to Shelley
        in his awful voyage
    as the Mayan Gods
        spears in hand
watch from a distance,
        and I cavort
            among the maidens.
I take myself there
            a visionary
    among tales of fortune
        and disillusionment.
And toss my soul
        like a madman
            trying to emulate
            scholarly diction,
    and flounder
        in the waves,
    ghost in the horizon.
    I toss these festered arms
            into political blunders

and poetic anarchy
professing a kinship
with the sea.
This bachelor of little eloquence
has a fate to surrender to
and in the quiet whispers
of morning,
walks with legendary
poetic heroes,
watching the sun rise
like a mother.
It takes a fool to be a poet;
an evil wonder lies at bay,
goodbye Mazatlan,
you have surrendered to me
like a woman,
throwing her blouse into the sea.

That My Name Is Omar

I suffer that my name is Omar Salinas.
That I want to touch someone in the
incredible loneliness of nights.
That I frighten away those I should
be close to. I suffer when I go crazy
and can't love anyone. Whether it
is Tuesday or Sunday, I suffer.
I suffer a lust for fame and
immortality. That I tried to
commit suicide. That I have
compassion for the unfortunate.
I suffer the death of matrimony.
The death of my mother.
The eyes of God.
I want to understand this and that
and come up with zero.
What should I do
but walk and look at the lovely sky?

Early Death

in memoriam Ben Durazo

The rain tonight
reminds me of you,
silent friend,
taken in the alabaster
tolling afternoon.
The sun was leaving—
only the sun comes back.

I feel like beating up philosophers,
or putting on a ghost's long shirt
to search you out in this tempest—
no use. No one wants anything
to do with the dead.

There,
in the afterlife,
your face will shine
like an orange moon.

Late Evening Conversation
with My Friend's Dog, Moses,
after Watching Visconti's *The Innocent*

Moses, who is there to save us
from the crickets, those small gods
in armor, nagging some vague truths
transient as Visconti's light
through the arbors of grape and lilac?
I think the loquats have been sleeping
like our guardian angels and
who is to say what the moon is thinking?
Or the lost fragments of our hearts?
It could all be the end of air
in liquor, rain, or self indulgence.
You could complain about each leaf
of the apricot, falling. I too
could catalog each woman that failed
to save me, and we both could be
as melancholy as clouds. Moses,
there are no prophecies in the sky,
only this earth, its grey at our
fingertips. Let's stop bitching
about death and the light of the lovers
on the veranda next door. I want
to explain, as you should too, about
the meekness of all the nights that
have passed, burnt-out stars or storms.
We must take control of the air
and breathe as only we can
like the icy throat of comets.
Listen to me Moses, we're not
as Biblical as rain, but our transgressions
go to the sea in search of speech.
Salt or otherwise, blood or otherwise,
things remain the same so long as we watch
the fiddles turn. And despite the women,
the rise and fall of French cinema,
the heart must dance like lightning,
burn, and save itself.

Salinas Summering
at the Caspian and Thinking of Hamlet

I get up and consider my corduroy coat
the collar tattered as Christianity;
they bring me several figs, a tangerine,
and rolls printed with a cross—
Is this what troubles are about?
I genuflect toward the sea,
whisper songs I learned in French
and throw crumbs to the seagulls
and anything hovering in the air.

There are boats with the red sails
of the past, and grey hulls approaching.
My pockets are thin and bulged as
a flatterer. As I put the coat on
I'm full of high sentence, or
I'm someone behind a curtain
overhearing the indiscretions
of the rich and courtly, or
the equal debate of flies.
I would have a play of sonorous maidens
asleep, orchids and gardenias
floating moon-like on the pond,
hearts left to the idiosyncrasies of youth . . .

Here the rivers are frozen,
the graves are dug in early spring;
my mind drifts to a courtyard
of children and their games against
the state. The next time I put on
my coat or hat and plan the downfall
or outcome of anything I'll have to
duel with the sunlight,
as pure as any of us
after the poisons and bad teeth
of love. What I want is a

white orange and the perpetual eye
of the glacier which sees one way
slowly and is blind to our tin
souls. Nevertheless, it's the snow
and my old shoes I glimpse at
like old women.

                    I step into it all
as if I were relieved of considerations
and the cacophony of mothers
admonishing us for our melancholy
hold on the wine glass—
this is something I know well among
the ice and small deposits of romance.
I know the blank music of the clouds
as well as I know my hands against
the window of my paramour—she is a
songless thrush and her cry is
the blue ink of night, the blood
returning to my heart with its air
beside the Caspian Sea, or any blue
far from here. I would meet her
and offer the inconsequence of
meager gloves at her breast,
the salt on our lips.

What else I ask myself do the rags
of flesh and minds ask for?
There is speech, and it comes now
in the form of swords or flames,
or it doesn't come at all.

Fragments for Fall

for Delmore Schwartz

September—
here I am, growing old
with the trees, bitter
about the lovely
ways of women
and the air hewn
with a light smoke
as they pass.

*

Lying in the park
with a squirrel
that's not afraid
of my hand,
imagining
a woman who's not afraid
of my life . . .
my feelings condense
like a cloud
about to go
into the blue.

*

I leave the house
with an umbrella
and one shoe,
and sing
in the grove
to the bankers
in their bowler hats.
I celebrate myself
in several newspapers
like a bear
at a honey log.

All morning
I'm Hamlet
mooning over history
and the voices
behind a row of elms
are mad as flies.

*

My feelings skip
like the wind
in a deaf tune
I roll in the grass,
some hero of the past
has a hand on
my throat.
This fear arrives
in the arms of violins
and Jew I remain,
standing in line
in a coat of moths,
in a coat of fog,
and the concert halts.

*

The early hour
tosses with
the semi-darkness
and tough shadows.
I reason
with my thumbs
and want to keep away
from obscure halls.
I can hear the cars
going perhaps everywhere,
golden in the early morning
and my friends sleep
the sleep of being close
to the museum.

*

Dead swans
drift in my imagination
and I take an early drink.

I take these legs
to dumbfounded churches
and weep for the fallen
god of mourning.
And the sunlight
hovers like smoke
over a train
carrying some poet's
bones, smiling
into the future
ahead of me.

*

I accuse the world
of having stolen
the pigeons from
my window,
and beneath the benches
feed them cocktail sandwiches
from the night before.
I am Schwartz
the magnanimous,
smooth of wit,
facile, glib, and true
as a meteor
in my castigations.

*

I am the best
of my age,
its hands and eyes,
and say so
while the clock ticks,
forlorn
as the frosted grass.

Letter to Leonard Adame

Now that the evening rain has gone
and a silence pervades like your arguments
against metaphysics, I conjure you
a theocrat in Tenochtitlan, smoothing the hair
of a princess or out searching the plaza
for the late delicacies of the night.
You call bird-like into the mist
and predict the migration of butterflies
with the silver notes of a flute;
the star of your eyes is dreaming ahead
to the calm prayer of the Spanish.
The moon sifts across your shoulders,
it is the coming of friendship into the house
of polemics and verse, and I purse my lips
like an Indian going out to the marketplace
for the first time in search of his brother.

Letter Left for Jon Veinberg

You must be out somewhere counting the trees or
the dreamers, the fireflies disappearing in October
with its treasures in a coat of dusk. I am welcomed
into your house by Moses, your dog, and the crickets
are serenading while the evening gathers its flesh
of children. I have wondered about Estonia, the blood
of your forefathers like a sky bluer than silence.
Under the stars I catch your warrior's laughter and
in the house of Estonia a last star traverses your eyes
in the hush of coffee and morning. You're a magician
in the clouds, sojourning through my life, a troubadour
singing the simple odes to light. I wish I could
spin your heart through my Mexican barrio and joke
the mariachi into song, quibble about girls and
the nature of angels. You are a song. And the ballads
of the mountain and cornfield sing a joy of good fortune
I too welcome dawn like you and whistle down the avenue,
confident, positive, the mid-noon sun will be a poem
written in the heart where it all belongs.

Soto Thinking of the Ocean

With the sun's
performance
dying slowly,
Soto thinks of
the ocean.

The powerful,
the weak
and the restless
inhabit
the shore
like drunk priests;
a puff of smoke
and a woman
full breasted
walks
the afternoon.

A crazy childhood
goes before us,
and Soto
is in the water again—
ointment
for youth,
old age
and belligerence,
blessings which
come our way
like goats
flushed from
the hills.
The ocean,
goddess,
immutable
temptress of water—
The incoming waves

catch us
in our
amazement,
that we are mortal,
that we could drown
near shore
and be remembered,
be recognized
like strong
tobacco,
and like pelicans
considered
in a strange way
romantics.
We are all being
beaten by the waves
under this
August sky.

You Are Not Here

for B.H.

And I piece together this friendship
like dusk finding its way through
the blue eucalyptus and touching my hand.
I see your face like Rembrandt perhaps
saw his mistress, and then walked outside
to stroll the streets. I can be honest
as this distance of ours shortens into love
and the blossoms twirl their tongues.
There is music to your voice and
a child's silence in your amber breasts.
I wait like a Parisian in a coffee shop
not wanting to waste words, words that
are like sparrows and fly deathless
into you, their mouths caught in the twigs
of their philosophy. I have to tell you
there is no one on the veranda
picking flowers or filling the birdbath.
And to what pains we've bitten into.
They're a bell of clouds in the memory,
dreams which snared us beneath the trees.
And the evening walks off, shrugging
its grey shoulders, and I'm on a bench
impetuous as the pigeons pecking
the nothings in my hands, holding
a simple hat for your soul.

Poem Before a Tremendous Drunk

I venture forth onto the avenue
like an avocado picker in search
of a woman. I am in an indelicate
cerebral mood, and the toxic
whispers of the starlings
keep my feet in bombastic
condition. I wish for once
to come upon this incredible
world and catch it by the nose,
toss it to the ground
and bedevil the evening
with young sarcasm.
Were I a novelist,
I would wire the nearest
telegraph office I was
working on my third masterpiece
to send more money.
But poetry is like a drunk
starling and must be met
head-on like the avocado
picker I was supposed to be,
the one searching for a Madonna
to help him keep up
with the extravagant
insignificance
of us all.

Darkness under the Trees

With a candle half lit from the kitchen,
a dark woman on the phone, a mad woman
thinking about romance, a Japanese girl
who comes up to my shoulders, and a
polite hunchback for company . . .
Desperation flashes his white teeth.
A pistol in the closet.
Any of us could go under the darkness
of trees. A black dog and a white
cat keep vigil. Our prayers go
unheard in this twilight where
the roses droop around the thickness
of flies and the stench of another day.
How I weep for the fallen
and their gentle steps
catching me like a camera
which cannot focus on pain.
The neighbors drunk on silence
and gritos! for Cinco de Mayo.
I wish I could explain to God,
ask forgiveness, but I'm awkward
with the sentimental.
Don Quixote and I have lost
our minds—this is
another involuntary jump
into the darkness under the trees . . .

Shoes

On this windy night
at a farm for losers
I imagine winners all night
drinking the night.
What a dismal day.
I want so much to look
the other way
but God won't let
me put on my shoes.

Lover in a Mad World

I'm the crazy lover
in a mad world,
surviving on the mire
of kisses and sacrifices.

I have a rendezvous
with opinions, the rain
and my unmarried love.

I have the fingers of sickness
and the heart of an oak.
The fire of my mother's brain
given the celestial wires.

I'm a witness to the deaths
of elegant women,
those dreamt up
and those self caused.

In New York I look
down the Avenue of The Americas
and there are no more dreams—
no stutter of butterflies,
not one unholy bosom.

I'm the rebel, angel, ghost
of a blue within—
haunted, evil, angry and
perplexed by the young,
trying to smile over the abyss
asking a Christian God
to save me.

Autumn

For Peter Everwine

Autumn again fluttering
silvery wings,
the finches gather
in the garden
like troubled peasants.
And I'm the peasant
without dreams
looking on—
Here all secrets
jump out of my head,
desperation plays
a distant violin.
Oh, that I were
a ghost dancing
a world of bells,
listening to the agony,
and a fistful
of tenderness
from my absent mother.

I Want to Tell You

I want to tell you
what you are for me,
girl with the feet
of my many childhoods.

Your mouth
is a blossom of vermillion,
pigeons fluttering
morning into light.

It would be wonderful
to catch you.

I want to disappear into a rose
and come back to you.
As the afternoon lifts, I
say what a hell of a life.
Your body of blue wind
makes me crazy. I want
to dissolve into the slow burn
of your eyes. Eyes that lead
to desire, pull and tug at my legs
like children at a cemetery.
Your waist of water,
I want to drown there.

But this morning's rain is quiet
and mournful like the breath
of a bird, and somehow I've
got to shake this sadness
away. I've got death caught
in my throat, like the bones
of a needlefish, backslapping
me into illusions.
I see my forty year old face
in the mirror, there's static

on the air but a laconic hush
in the eyes.
My mother would be proud
to know my thirst for life
is finding its words.

This May Morning

Someone is mowing the lawn
in the distance.
I am looking at a bunch
of cows wag their tails.
My schizophrenic friend
is thumbing through the mail,
a sudden, half-hidden terror
in his eyes.
The trees are
restless, I'm restless, and
the whole world is like
an old kettle drum,
moving slowly and capriciously.
The roosters are crowing.
The wind comes like a messenger
from the east, wishing us
all happy birthdays . . .

We're like a hopeless
bunch of rats
caught in their traps.
And Jesus in abeyance,
we're all thieves here.
The train is elegant,
easing our pains.
I wish we were on it.
All the mad need
is a ride somewhere.
And Beauty, she's off
somewhere taking a bath.
And I'm secretly hoping
for two days of rain.

A Fresh Start

I begin to tell it . . .
this morning breaks into my life
like a bleak pale stranger
who wants nothing, and begs
for life as if it added up
to something. And the silence
grows immaculate in my fingers
wanting to touch someone tender.
I wonder if love
is like an apertif
turning one into a drunk
or some tubercular ghost
suddenly appearing.
I grieve the melancholy
of swallows and how the persimmon
tree outside is like an only child,
and I'm aware I'm alone.
And I'm walking sideways
in my many childhoods,
anarchist and lonely hunter
of the dark.
I could be saved from it all
but the clouds have nothing to say.
And my loves are so distant
that I must have made this story up.

This Is What I Said

"I'm a very metaphysical cat,
someday I'll be slicing apples
in heaven," I tell my companion
the Estonian. The night
is just right for this, and
he laughs, and we both laugh.
Deep inside me, I think
difficult thoughts and wonder
whether my intellect is sharp
enough for this, or if I can
translate the feeling that
overcame me when my grandfather died,
or the time I had a high fever
and saw ghosts in the garden
and my mother consoled me.

There was a time when I chased
butterflies in Mexico, and the
mad nearby grinned with huge
faces which seemed to be made
of my mother's apron.
I realize I'm nothing;
yet if something kind were
to come from nowhere,
I'd start believing all over
again, and smile at a girl's
fancifulness, gather myself,
and make a life.

The Odds

When the odds are against you
all you have to do is grin . . .
How does a man of substance
learn to divide and subtract?
But by paying attention
and simply trying. How does
anyone do anything? Even animals
have customs; I only wish
they could ask a perfect
question like what time is it?
or, when do I have to go to bed?
Going to bed is difficult, especially
if you don't have someone dear . . .

Let the dead-mad divide and
anger the moon, but I prefer
to simply go unadorned
among kings and hold my head
high among the common towns
I come from, unnoticed in my
open coat and summer hat.
I've known dogs in my life
who have died gallantly
with feet straight up in the air.

The Woman Who Follows Me Home from the Park

I go to the park I love
where women in black
relax like forgotten madonnas,
and I talk to myself
in Spanish.

The sun leaves a piece
of gloom at twilight;
immersed in blue thought,
smoke trails me

to a bar where a woman
is putting on lipstick,
trying to avoid the tragedy
of the juke box and mirrors.
We sing to swallows
on their way to the graveyard
over silver martinis,

and soon I am fondling
a breast
on a mountain of bone;
the woman is ashen-faced,
the flower of evening
smelling of snow.

In the yellow dust
beyond the door,
girls dance
and carry smiles to town,
I groan under the bills of
mockingbirds,
twirl my tongue and whistle.

A wild guitar plays
over a green hill.
I separarate my fingers
and lust flies
on black horses' hooves
by the road.

After I'm Gone

The room will smell of olives
and oleanders.
I will want to wake up
and see the rain,
touch some faces with my fingertips,
and apologize.
I will want music.
I will want to kiss the earth
and take my eyes to a Mexican
cemetery.

But the air will be blue,
my loved one will be dressed
in black, soused, and in tears.
On the far side of town
will be a band headed for the madhouse.
My sons and daughters will
by playing games.

The pages of my manuscripts
will blow loose
and turn into flies.
Everyone will be killing flies
and I'll be a romantic
again dreaming about crazy women
dressed in red.
I'll be quietly dreaming
again after I'm gone.

Walking Behind The Spanish

The Road of El Sueño by the Sea

Thinking of the silent deaths by the sea
and of the beautiful women in Santa Barbara,
I stroll backwards into the heavens
of my soldier's face, poor aristocrat
in a town with too much money.
I secretly run my hand up a Greek
woman's bosom and drink to those
secrets that will never be mine.
I spun in crazy here looking for
the kharma I lost elsewhere.
A gentle ghost haunts the Taverna.
Have I discovered myself here?
Death looms in the distance
with bent ears, I'm going around
circles begging the night
to return to Santa Barbara
where the future
sways its fingertips,
and where we will be on the road
of El Sueño humming this
evening, the dream will be gone,
and the sea, the quiet bystander
to all this, will begin
to tune itself to a quiet madness.

My Dead Friends Are Hitchhiking

This day in September with the black
angels of death hovering above like dark mistresses,
my dead friends are hitchhiking and ghosts
in the countryside dance.
I'm a passenger on a bus on the way
to the madhouse to see someone.
It's all familiar my coming here
the voice that said "All will be well,"
and the dark stranger who swore
Jesus would be back.
My friend is in another world preparing
for the next war. Should I tell him he
is already in one, that someone is going
to cover him with a sheet and not give
a damn. That his goings and comings
are for naught. Friend, on this day
I could write you a poem and you
couldn't understand. "No one understands,"
I mumble. I catch his eye; he knows.
The doomed shall be saved.

I Surrender in the March of My Bones

I surrender in the march of my bones
to another night, and am stung
by the air which hums
delicately my name.
These words coming as confused
larks to play games.
These hands
which are like spiders to my being
used to the lonely
alienation of their web.
I am here night and day
in the fragrance
of the crazy air,
in the shadow of the ghettos
in the awkward palm
of poverty.
Alone, I see
coffins with sails
and winter's ghost
walks on the pier.
The lovely women who must die
like broken dolls
and the hummingbird
with its
feminine heart
on the edge of insanity.
I surrender to the march of my bones
to another day,
which feels for my throat
like the lost feet
of a nightingale.
Inwardly I listen to the trembling
of the utter silence
and that life is passing
like a magician scattering stars.

Women Like Taverns I've Dreamt

I am a cow
and I am chasing you.
Soon I will turn
into a swan
and kiss
you.
If I pretend
long enough
I will eat you
raw,
then look for
you
somewhere in
my shoe.
If you're good
I'll look
inside
your eyes,
pass out
on your breasts
and ride a train
to the cemetery
where they will
bury all of us
like damned souvenirs
someone forgot
to open.
In the meantime
a haunted woman
lures me
to her house
where a drunk
pigeon
hums lullabyes
and her lust
points at me
like the fingernail
of death.

I Salute the Dead

In this drunken town
bitten by the whores
of Texas, I pause with
a beer to salute the dead.

Someone's in my house
—the dead child of Texas
haunts the woodwork
and the child is everywhere
tonight waiting for the dawn,
tomorrow maybe playing
in the mud.

My nephew asks if the black
children he sees on TV
are the poor, and I reply,
"We are the poor."
He cannot understand,
and I know this house
is as poor as this drunken
town
and I drink my beer and
hiccup into song.

Falling and Remembering

Listening this gray Tuesday
to little philosophers, finches—
rebels who gather each morning
reminding me of the dead.
I am here like an introverted
rose, stoic, quiet in bloom,
knowing the petals will fall
like some drunk in a cantina.
Afternoon too is falling
like a tiny God with no name,
and I'm falling and the slow
wind is bending the shoots
of plants like my heart thinking
of dying. There is no escape—
a fly buzzes my ear reminding
me I must stop this.

A Bit Crazy

I'm growing fonder
of the light
which has pierced
this heart of olives.
Like a huge hand
that wears shoes,
like a lighthearted woman
out to the opera.
Darkness has scattered my clothes,
my poems.
Evening salutes
like an admiral,
my heart is among the trees
in laughter.
I leave my solitude
holding on
like a scared prostitute,
and amble on
a little stage frightened,
the world looking on,
the small applause of stars,
as my heart tips its hat . . .

Rosita, the Future Waits with Hands of Swans

To the vile drumbeat of evening
dressed in fine silks
to an awkward offbeat
a wave of ocean water,
I escape among the little gods
of moonlight the castaway.
To the kiss of the imaginative
woman, the hard knock
of her eyes, the petulant
grief imbedded in is all—
I smile, the tolerant
hellish gesticulator
of the brainy night.
In whose hands we do
leave that softness,
killing us.
In what twist
do I leave Rosita
whose life batters
the insane flies of romanticism.
In whose blood do we sing?
And what if the moon sent
a messenger with round
impetuous eyes to take
our hands?
Rosita's bloody wrists
the trumpet blares in her eardrums.
Do I listen to this cumbia
or do I take my Aztec
hands to forecast
the future intelligence
of Cuauhtemocs.
I shall find you in Tocalitlan,
my. Mexican wife,
in a very gorgeous gown.
Rosita, face to face,
what will you tell me?

My Quixotic Bang Up

(The tragedy which broke me open)

There is a full moon
tonight and I am
as confused as
the lark.
Could it be
because
the moon houses
the mad?
Or is it
loneliness
stretched out
on the porch
like a cat.
I am in this labor
of life tasting
a resin
which is unlike a woman.
I lite a cigarette—
the moon looks like
it is in terrible pain,
the insides of trees
are bleeding,
this house
is going to be eaten by darkness,
the dogs are as sad
as the last oranges of winter,
and I'm coming back from it.
Back from the temptress
back from the mad.
I am a romantic
but I've had it up to my ears
listening to the damned.
I want no more madness

Lord.
That suffering
of imbecilic
homicidal moons,
that rebellion of stars
in the quiet nights
of searching.
I who want the depth
of harmony
have found compassion
among the deaf
and crazy;
now with the road
winding its fingers
like a composer,
I poeticize
the gentle spirit
of this quixotic bang up.

Someone Is Buried

for Federico Garcia Lorca

The children are going to the clouds
to hear flamenco,
and there's a loud roar in heaven, Lorca.

They're still firing bullets, damnit,
and the world's on fire.

Women are passing, counting the dead—
horsemen with knives in the thicket.

Someone is being buried.
Black ribbons under an anonymous moon
and the wrong face under our blessings.

In heaven an angel fixes his trousers.
in Granada, the bells are tolling.

Someone is being buried.
There is no marker on your grave
in Granada, Federico Garcia Lorca.

I'm Walking Behind the Spanish

eavesdropping on their conversation:
Neruda sound asleep,
Juan Ramon placing yellow flowers
in his kitchen.
Miguel in jail.
Lorca playing flamenco
to a house full of romanceros.
Cesar Vallejo walking through
the streets of Paris.
I walk behind you
carrying this heart
of white rain which has
come out of the barrio
with the turbulence of
the Guadalquivir.
The sun is a witness
to your coming and going
like soldiers marching
towards the sea.
And this petty inquisitive
brain has watched you
enter my life.
Miguel weeping.
Lorca clean shaven and alert
murdered standing.
Neruda calm like dropping fruit.
Juan Ramon Jimenez
in a portrait of yellow flowers.
And Vallejo drunk with the ghost
of compassion, sipping cold coffee.

            *

Behind time I'm
like a lost finger
in the sea.
Thrashing about
looking for a lost heaven.

I go dizzy through the crowds
whispering a tender
folktale as if to a ghost.
I'm taking everything
to the sea, toss bird bones
there, eat bread and hold on.

*

I'm walking behind
the Spanish in a Madrigal
dream.
The Cow lays down,
the worker goes home
to his wife of complaints.
The banker can't spend
his money.

*

I lead a tragic life
but I have the optimism of
the owl.
Forlorn diplomat
of my existence
I go in soldier fashion
through life—
scarred, foolish
and romantic.
Making the best
of what is there.
And feel the tug
of angels in my footsteps.

I Live Among the Shadows

With the backdrop
of lovers in the meadows,
this beaten heart
asking to be dropped
like fruit from
a tree,
I go again
into the shuffle
of my mind,
somewhat weatherbeaten,
carrying a shadow
through the fields . . .

This is the fictional
rendition of my life—
I am the blind organ player,
none of the keys are white,
none black, the music
somewhere in between . . .

And when I think
of the afterlife,
a trail of breadcrumbs
leads back to itself,
fattening the grey birds
that ask nothing of me
but circle all day
in the near, blue distance . . .
sometimes I think I
could throw a stone,
a coin, the silver bracelet
with my name, sometimes,
my shirt is no defense,
and the birds are vague
as an itch on the lover's
backs in the field, or stars

behind the clouds of night,
sometimes they are as vague
as my eyes, as the one road
of the lost, as my empty hands . . .
I must have left something,
somewhere.

Letter too late to Vallejo

This is the letter that couldn't get to you
because you were looking for food in Paris.
To your frail October bones I phrase my lines
like spokes in your heart of silver, and condemn
loneliness, fools, idle walkers through an immense rain.
There is a crimson hue to your cloud, bloodless
in the sky and giving like a child. There is a pallor
on your forehead the years won't take away
and a huge meteor circling the night of insomnia,
and you're taciturn, a quiet constellation of grit
and hope in the vapor of one more night alone.
Your Peruvian soul grieves like a cistern in a warehouse
of love, and the toxic moody eyes of one who's seen hell
and disappeared to heaven on the arithmetic of air.
You never returned to Peru, the university where
your fervid muscles ached like stars on their way
to jail. I see your hunger and metaphysical black angels
working around you and an impulse says, "Everything
will end soon on a Thursday in the rain."

Ode to Cervantes

You who died poor
tasting the very juices of fame
hero of war and philosophy,
the barroom and brothel,
the dungeon and Spanish stars.

This night of utter misfortune
and misery I want to pay homage
to your creation, your orphan,
your son—
that gentle knight of madness
using his helmet as a soup bowl
like any shining itinerant.

Miguel Saavedra Cervantes
brawler of the countryside.
My saint this connubial
blundered night
of catastrophic mistakes
and a tilted will.

I want to take you to my heart
find a vein of poetry there
and follow it like the Guadalquivir
through the widowed plains

I of sound mind
and wind in my logic
want to go against the State,
be imprisoned there,
and give compassion
to the luminous underdogs.

Let them speak of asylums,
of ghosts, of pain and rejection—
let God give us the constant struggle,
bread, and pursuit of dreams.

Cervantes, I want to touch
your bones and not bitch
about poverty anymore.

God is with me.
My friends are with me,
even if the people do not know
of this sadness,
which has built a path
inside my soul
on which I've traveled up and down
wrestling the white ghost of literature
and aristocratic circles.

I follow you through little towns
with heartaches and ballads
in their church steeples,
those roads of woe,
the holy gardens and cantinas
of lost design, ladies,
and the magnanimous folly
beneath a huge and wonderful sky.

Ode to Miguel Hernandez

Sitting quietly by the rivers
of summer, I pause and think,
"The Spanish are gathering their
speech in the clouds." The rustle
of trains backing into your soul
and those awful brooms standing
corpselike in the courtyard of
prisons, have no use for your
poems with their dove flight
to everywhere. No, not even your
bones on the neck of a bull would
begin to forget. I blame the
evening like a malignant stranger
straying into a battlefield, with
the blood of snow melting your
mouth into forgotten fields of
poppies. And those trains
of the wounded, bound and gauzed
in purple clouds exclaiming
the Republic. On a day like this
you are walking through the countryside
with Ramon Sije, writing your betrothed
and not realizing an end
to all your prismatic dreams.
I take your sheepherder's speech
and make a prayer in July,
and damn misfortune, brooms, silences,
and go with the pain into the storm,
and with this ode, forget myself . . .

As I Look to the Literate

With small steps of amazement,
I go foolish into life,
foggy brained with the music
of oblique miracles.
The facts are plain, leatherminded
and scallawagged, but sensing
greater truths from them,
I am glimpsed at from
without—and a sure-footed
Cervantes lives in me
a wispy spider's flight.
Pleased with the nonsense
I've conjured, the night
air falls into my
lap of dreams.
As I fill this heart with
this dry language,
I focus
on the ordinary mathematics
of living, and go about my business
like a serious man
with a pencil behind
my ears.

When the Stars Get Angry
and Coo above Our Heads for the
Generation of Spanish Civil War Poets

When the stars coo above
our heads like stragglers
in the sky and the birds
talk a strange language
I think of the absent.
Like a stranger
walking the streets
with the wounded
eyes of the swallow
I talk to absence.
They are gone
and the countryside
lies bare
before me
like a missing child
some metaphor
dumbstruck in a Spanish
ballad.
Death struck like a bone
in the wind knocking
senselessly about.
It took Cesar
In the crazy insomniac
night.
It bit Lorca in pieces
under the Falangist moon.
It walked into Juan Ramon
like a woman wanting romance.
It crawled
from an immense crevice
in the earth
and chose Miguel.
It lunged at Neruda
like a barefoot

accordionist.
When the stars coo
above our heads,
the absent are about
and the strange sound
in the evening
looks at the nude heart
of poetry in the bare
corners of all our rooms.

The Ghost of Emiliano Zapata

This Sunday at the Market
with the clouds
like guerillas,
and the people
dove-like
approaching
as if from
the mountains,
the ghost of Emiliano
Zapata haunts
the market place.
This Sunday
the churches
are markers
for graves,
and the insane
silence
rides a horse
to some heaven.
The woman across from
me wants to
be a mother
and I am full
of ambition.
The multiplication
        table of the poor
begins here
and the multiplication
of the dead ends
here as well.
Life on all fours
gets up
and lifts
itself like
a tired woman.
A hush enters
my lungs peopled
with darkness.

When This Life No Longer Smells of Roses

It will be raining,
the air will be blue,
my compadres will be
singing rancheras
and seagulls will be
dancing the "Jarabe."
My loved one will come
all the way from Paris;
my creditors will
denounce me.
Children will be
thrashing piñatas
and in the barrio
they will be singing
"Por Una Mujer Casada."
A would-be nun
will slash her wrists.
A gypsy will have
his guitar stolen.
My poems will turn up
in Mazatlan, starched
as napkins in good cafes,
and I'll be rehearsing
a ballad by Negrete,
dreaming of villages,
the white breasts
of the sea, and there will
be plenty of laughter.
When this life no longer
smells of roses,
I'll have left
on a tour with Don Quixote—
I'll leave no forwarding
address.

My Father Is a Simple Man

I walk to town with my father
to buy a newspaper. He walks slower
then I do so I must slow up.
The street is filled with children.
We argue about the price
of pomegranates, I convince
him it is the fruit of scholars.
He has taken me on this journey
and it's been lifelong.
He's sure I'll be healthy
so long as I eat more oranges,
and tells me the orange
has seeds and so is perpetual;
and we too will come back
like the orange trees.
I ask him what he thinks
about death and he says
he will gladly face it when
it comes but won't jump
out in front of a car.
I'd gladly give my life
for this man with a sixth
grade education, whose kindness
and patience are true . . .
The truth of it is, he's the scholar,
and when the bitter-hard reality
comes at me like a punishing
evil stranger, I can always
remember that here was a man
who was a worker and provider,
who learned the simple facts
in life and lived by them,
who held no pretense.
And when he leaves without
benefit of fanfare or applause
I shall have learned what little
there is about greatness.

I Am America

It's a hell of a world.
I go like a schoolboy stepping
through the murderous countryside,
a bit of rhyme, a little drunk
with the wonderful juices of breasts,
and the magnificent
with their magician-like words
slipping into the voice of America.
I carry my father's coat,
some coins,
my childhood eyes in wonder—
the olive trucks plucky
in their brash ride
through the avenue,
the wino in a halo of freedom,
the shopkeepers of Democracy.

I am brave, I am sad
and I am happy with the workers in the field,
the pregnant women
in ten dollar dresses,
the night air supping
and stopping to chat
like a wild romantic lady.
Children's voices and dogs,
the bar, the songs and fights.
I go ruminating in the brothels,
the ghettos, the jails.
Braggart, walking into early
cafes confessing naivete
and love for the unemployed.
I'm a dream in the land
like the Black, Mexican, Indian,
Anglo and Oriental faces
with their pictures of justice.
I go gaudy into movie houses,
flamboyant spectator

of horse races.
I am not unloved, or unwanted
but I have seen the faces
of the rebel, the outcast,
I have touched the madness, all the terrible
and I have seen the ghosts of the past.
I am a friend to all,
for I have touched everything,
even the empty plates of the poor.

I put on my clothes, my hat,
I visit everywhere—
I go to market for bananas,
smoke the air,
breathe America.

I am wretched and mean,
I am kind and compassionate.
I remember catechism class,
the nuns and the priests,
my sister's wit,
and the neighbor's beautiful wife.
I am walking behind America,
suspicious, pie-eyed,
open-faced in the distance.
I am a father of prayers,
obedient,
I am a father of women,
a son of women.
I speak as the common man
and listen like the wise.
I am America,
and by hearts grown cold to me
I will be the seer of my intellect.
I will put an end to misery with
the bravado of the seeker,
drunken, reveling
in this American continent,
tight fisted,
exposed like a blue rose
to the night stars.

The Sadness Of Days

Come Pick Up My Body

Come pick up the body, the fingers will tell you.
Come with the quickness of deer,
Jumping over a tooth.
This afternoon is inside a box, in tears,
And I'm lunching beside a woman
With a small dog and too many words.
I am in a silly housecoat, as if day and night
Were lovers, as if this loneliness had a cat's tail,
As if madness were a drunk neighbor
Or a dog on fire. Come and pick up the body,
The hands will guide you
Into a furnace of laughter, into the fired heart.
Come with the freedom of a katydid, of open eyes.
Come like the aunt who was thinking
Of an apron before she died.
I will sit by your table, sullen and a bit fearful
For that is all of me.
Come for I will drink and forget you.
Come pick up the body, my sadness will tell you.

Back in Town Again

With clouds dying in the sky
I accept the past year
of boredom and sit
in my polished brown coat
and grin at the workers
shuffling off in their turbulence.
I am convinced
Hell has no back door—
all we can do is breathe
and not push too hard.

The mad peacock flutters,
the finch, the cats and dogs
walk and stare
with the midnoon sun.
And my anger has a face
I don't want to see,
the victrola ringing
country western
and the years pass
like limousines.
I count my living friends,
pause at a grave,
button my coat
and light a cigarette
to the women
that encircle me
like puddles of beer.

My mother lights a candle
at church and I'm her friend
again. My father is losing
his sight, but the spirit
is stubborn as milkweed
commanding the earth.
And I stand in a corner
a little happier, looking
through the trees,
walking softly into town.

The Sadness of Days

I've been sad for days.
Not with the sadness of being born,
or the sadness of a torn romance.
But with the sadness of a poor man smiling.
Honestly I would like to feel compassion
for those without luck.
I would like to touch their suffering
and say that I understand.
These days in November are obscure,
almost silver, and given to the heavens.
Honestly I want to find myself,
to sit under a tree with its dusty fruit
of salvation. I will take my place,
Listen up, and have faith in all things.

Letter to Soto

We're, on our way alright, with a herd
Of wild dogs, for I have been
Frightened by the city.
So go to the hills to be renewed—
Even the sky is different.
The stars huddle like women,
And I am counting my sighs
For there is much to be said
About wealth. We're on our way alright—
The river where you almost drowned,
And Mariko exclaiming, "I'm from the plum
Country." Certainly the ghettos walk
On bad knees. The Fresno prostitutes
Are trying to convince us to look up their sleeves.
The beggars bumping into me with eyes of pale milk.
And a woman somewhere, whispering
To the lilacs, "Omar is crazy."
Yes, ladies, yes, yes, yes to anything.
And the big theater of loneliness,
Like a huge hand dropping out of the sky.
Yet, I can hear my friends in the distance,
Like doves saying, "Omar,
it's alright, it's alright."
And the mind adds zeros. The flesh talks of youth
And its heart. The heart is silent,
Like the dangling string on the package
Of cigarettes in the asylum.
And they find me on bad elbows by the meadow
With a copy of Omar Khayyam, whiskey,
And my poems that can't find an ear.

Beyond the Sea

(at the sanatorium)

One with the eyes of a sufferer.
One with the face of milk.
The saddest one looks for God.
The others forget.
Gertrude in the nude in her room,
Waiting.
The one beyond help doesn't know
Gertrude like I do.
And Paul faces the wall.
They're bringing in drinks.
What dreams lay here,
Like broken ships
The sea won't forget.

And this ship of the lost won't move.
Only John and Gertrude move
and it's like a long dip
In the ocean.
Their bodies are pressed together
Like something from the sea—
Making the small noises
Of whales that have no end.

It Will Be Darkness Soon

It will be darkness soon
and she will be slipping into bed
like an angelfish. I gaze
out the window and observe
the quiet in the revery of the trees.
I am reminded of a sad uncle
who drank whiskey and died
sitting on a stool.
The woman's beauty will also fade
into an abandonment.
As I think through these lines
she wakens and calls.
I touch her shoulder
and remember the sea,
the solitude of a rising moon
saying the heart has always drifted
and it will be darkness soon.

Melancholy

Merely to gaze at her like a tired acrobat.
She sits by the window like a colorful minnow.
Who will catch her, woo her to the dance?

Who can understand what is inside
those large eyes? The snake of Irony?
The man takes off his shirt, his shoes.
She merely looks up like water, and sighs.

They invent a garden where he will pick flowers.
And he will run after something
and come back with one eye.

And he will cry out like a hounded hound.
And the clouds move above like a sinister piano.
It will be raining and a hard silence follows.

Among the Flowers

Talk to me that I may understand.
For my fingers burn to hear
that I will find love in a subway,
that I will be entertained by crickets
until I break into dream and stop running.
Talk to me so I will not look at my corpse
or whistle on the dark edge of my boot.
Sing if you can to my solitary hat
discovering me again. Walk with me
without letting on you're a stranger
and I a cripple, bound in gauze
for the evening. Tell everyone I was here
with an overpowering illusion,
bowing my head, pausing among
the ample sorrow of irises.

Pain

Come with me,
discuss philosophy.
I'm tired of looking
at the unbent trees.
Take these eyes
to a celebration
where I'll forget who
I am.
Come with me.
tell my neighbor poverty
to quit knocking,
for I am alone
and getting ready to weep.
And the day has just begun
to count its pennies.
Introduce yourself to my shoes
for you will find them
to be scuffed and friendly.
Come, I implore you
to eat at my table
before you turn into a woman
and wreck my life.

Until Daybreak

It is evening,
clouded and still.
My fingers shout,
no one can hear them.
No one can see me
outfitted in the color of dusk.
Shadows dart in the backyard
in the criminal air,
and a woman could die here,
pull out her hair and die.

My hobo heart plays cards,
the dogs bark at the devil.
I am back in the intestines
of a small town.
Cover me with your love
in the dark page of sleep.
Single out my face.
I will be the keeper of silence.
I will beat these drums of night air.

In Life

I am interested in the happiness of birds,
their quiet pose in the backyard—
and the voice of a hero in jovial freedom.
In my circle of life I've learned something
of a deep sadness, how troubadours bring
greetings of joy from the afterlife.
They are quick to recognize me.
I become sadder when my face
inhabits the discolored sun,
when the owl and the rabbit are wounded
and go off to die with no music but the winds.
The Mexican song my father listens to says,
"I will not return."
Father, your son loves you.
In the coffee shop I know your sight is failing
for you can't recognize your friends
and your coins. Now the days are long
and we grow restless. Think of it when you go,
your son has his heart on poems
that will clean up the image of death.
With our guts, death won't bother us.
But when you lost your father
and when he lost his, there was a deadening
of life in the fields, a flattened rabbit,
blackbirds like leaves in the dry sycamore,
and your lucid eyes filled me with wonder.
The old do not have much to live for
but we've made gains.

Don't worry father, I'll be quiet around you,
for carrying grief is not supposed to be our way.
I'll just go and be generous with my anger.
I'll be tightlipped, drink from your brandy,
eye a woman and tell her I've seen Paris . . .
We've done it all you and I, and certainly
these are not tears that are in my eyes,
only a handfull of dust blowing
as in all of life. We'll say goodbye father,
with a gutty magnificence.

In the Thick of Darkness

When night comes in
I will be a startled crab
in the thick of darkness.
I will be ancient
and likewise young.
When dusk rolls in
rabbit-eared and cockeyed,
I will surround myself
with my old friend, solitude.
When night kneels
like a beggar
I will surprise a woman
and put a knife
into joy—
its blood of mercy
might well save me.
I shall be gone for days
carrying the sack of desire,
and from the laconic provinces
I will rise clean shaven
wearing the hard crust
of silence.

On a Visit to a Halfway House after a Long Absence

I am here bright eyed
and night is here also
with its cold and awful memories.
No news is brought here
that will save anybody.
The damned and the defeated
share coffee here
like lost apostles, but
no saint or prayer can
change the hunger or the cold.
Winter and the devil
have conspired,
for to step into madness
has its wry smell
and romance . . .
I leave this place and its
aroma of suicides, for the lost
have gathered here
like wounded sparrows;
and the inhuman
and the human
suffocate in this air,
in this terrible refuge.

How Much Are You Worth

Come sit with poverty for an hour.
Capitalism is a large room with idiotic stares.
And seagulls might as well recite the rosary.
Money that runs its hand over your face.
Anger that does not approach justice.
Come sit by the Martyrs of the highway.
Tie the shoelace of the beggar.
Come make yourself useful.
Boil an egg. Fry some cheese.
Run after Senators—stop their cars.
Wash the feet of the poor.